The
BLESSED
MOTHER

The
BLESSED
MOTHER

Designed by Liz Trovato
Compiled by Gwynn Hayes

GRAMERCY BOOKS
New York • Avenel

For their help, advice, and contributions to this book I thank Sue Malone Barber, Brigit Enriquez, Romeo Enriquez, Carol Kelly Gangi, Lillian Guzzo, William Huelster, Gwen Kelly, Donna Lee Lurker, Jeanne Mosure, Horace Whyte, and, for the concept and much encouragement, Harold Clarke.

G.H.

This edition is published by Gramercy Books,
distributed by Random House Value Publishing, Inc.
40 Engelhard Avenue
Avenel, New Jersey 07001

Random House
New York • Toronto • London • Sydney • Auckland

Printed and bound in China

Library of Congress Cataloging-in-Publication Data

The Blessed Mother/edited by Gwynn Hayes.
p. cm.
ISBN 0-517-12441-6
1. Mary, Blessed Virgin, Saint,--Literary collections.
I. Hayes, Gwynn.
PN6071.M27B54 1995
808.8'0351--dc20   95-17659 CIP

8 7 6 5 4 3 2 1

EHOLD, THE VIRGIN SHALL CONCEIVE, AND BEAR A SON, AND SHALL CALL HIS NAME IMMANUEL.

ISAIAH 7: 14

No woman that ever lived on the face of the earth has been an object of such wonder, admiration, and worship as Mary the mother of Jesus.

Around her poetry, painting, and music have raised clouds of ever-shifting colors, splendid as those around the setting sun. Exalted above the earth, she has been shown to us as a goddess, yet a goddess of a type wholly new. She is not Venus, not Minerva, not Ceres, nor Vesta.

No goddess of classic antiquity or of any

other mythology at all resembles that ideal being whom Christian art and poetry present to us in Mary. Neither is she like all of them united. She differs from them as Christian art differs from classical, wholly and entirely. Other goddesses have been worshipped for beauty, for grace, for power. Mary has been the Goddess of Poverty and Sorrow, of Pity and Mercy.

In Mary, womanhood, in its highest and tenderest development of the mother, has been the object of worship.

HARRIET BEECHER STOWE

And the angel come in unto her and said Hail, thou that art highly favored; the Lord is with thee; blessed are thou among women. Fear not, Mary, for thou has found favor with God. And behold, thou shalt conceive in thy womb and bring forth a son, and thou shalt call his name Jesus.

Luke 1: 28, 30, 31

The Magnificat

My soul doth magnify the Lord:
And my spirit hath rejoiced
 in God my Savior.
Because He hath regarded the lowliness
 of His Handmaid:
  for, behold, from henceforth all
  generations shall call me blessed.
For He that is mighty hath done great things
  to me: and holy is His Name.
And His mercy is from generation
 unto generations,
  to them that fear Him.

He hath showed might with His arm:
      He hath scattered the proud
      in the conceit of their heart.
He hath put down the mighty from their seat,
      and hath exalted the lowly.
He hath filled the hungry with good things:
      and the rich He hath
      sent empty away.
He hath received Israel His servant,
      being mindful of His mercy;
As He spoke to our fathers, to Abraham and
      to his seed forever.

LUKE 1:46–55

. . . AND MARY
SAID . . . "I AM
THE HANDMAID
OF THE LORD;
LET IT BE TO ME
ACCORDING TO
YOUR WORD."

LUKE 1:31, 38

Lowliest of women, and most glorified:
In thy still beauty, sitting calm and lone:
A brightness round thee grew; and by thy side,
Kindling the air, a form ethereal shone,
Solemn, yet breathing gladness.
From her throne a queen had risen with more
        imperial eye;
A stately prophetess of victory
From her proud lyre had struck a tempest's tone.
For such high tidings as to thee were brought,
Chosen of heaven, that hour: but thou, O thou,
E'en as a flower with gracious rains o'er fraught,
Thy Virgin head beneath its crown didst bow,
And take to thy meek breast the All-holy Word,
And own thyself the handmaid of the Lord.

FELICIA D. HEMANS

Mary set out, proceeding in haste into the hill country of Judah, where she entered Zachariah's house and greeted Elizabeth. When Elizabeth heard Mary's greeting, the baby leapt in her womb. Elizabeth was filled with the Holy Spirit . . . "Blessed is she who trusted that the Lord's words to her would be fulfilled." And Mary said: "My soul proclaims the greatness of the Lord."

St. Luke 1:39-41, 45-46

Regina Coeli

Say, did his sisters wonder what could
    Joseph see
In a mild, silent little maid like thee?
And was it awful in that narrow house,
With God for Babe and Spouse?
Nay, like they simple, female sort, each one
Apt to find Him in Husband and in Son,
Nothing to thee came strange in this.
They wonder was but wondrous bliss:
Wondrous, for, though
True Virgin lives not but does know,
(Howbeit none ever yet confess'd)
That God lies really in her breast,
Of thine He made His special nest
And so
All mothers worship little feet,
And kiss the very ground they've trod;
But, ah, thy little Baby sweet
Who was indeed thy God!

Coventry Patmore

And she brought forth

her firstborn son, and wrapped him

in swaddling clothes

and laid him in a manger.

Luke 2:7

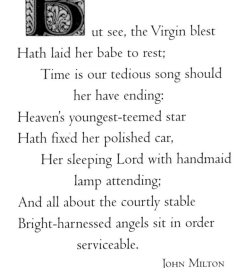

ut see, the Virgin blest
Hath laid her babe to rest;
　　Time is our tedious song should
　　　　her have ending:
Heaven's youngest-teemed star
Hath fixed her polished car,
　　Her sleeping Lord with handmaid
　　　　lamp attending;
And all about the courtly stable
Bright-harnessed angels sit in order
　　　　serviceable.

JOHN MILTON

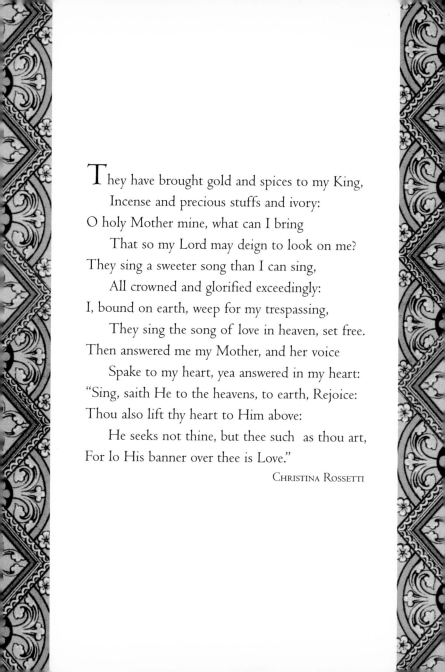

They have brought gold and spices to my King,
    Incense and precious stuffs and ivory:
O holy Mother mine, what can I bring
    That so my Lord may deign to look on me?
They sing a sweeter song than I can sing,
    All crowned and glorified exceedingly:
I, bound on earth, weep for my trespassing,
    They sing the song of love in heaven, set free.
Then answered me my Mother, and her voice
    Spake to my heart, yea answered in my heart:
"Sing, saith He to the heavens, to earth, Rejoice:
Thou also lift thy heart to Him above:
    He seeks not thine, but thee such as thou art,
For lo His banner over thee is Love."

CHRISTINA ROSSETTI

THE STAR WHICH THEY HAD OBSERVED AT ITS RISING WENT AHEAD OF THEM UNTIL IT CAME TO A STANDSTILL OVER THE PLACE WHERE THE CHILD WAS. THEY WERE OVERJOYED AT SEEING THE STAR, AND ON ENTERING THE HOUSE, FOUND THE CHILD WITH MARY HIS MOTHER. THEY PROSTRATED THEMSELVES AND DID HIM HOMAGE. THEN THEY OPENED THEIR TREASURES AND PRESENTED HIM WITH GIFTS OF GOLD, FRANKINCENSE AND MYRRH.

ST. MATTHEW 2:9-11

Sleep, sleep, mine Holy One,
My flesh, my Lord—what name? I do not know
A name that seemeth not too high, or low,
    Too far from me, or heaven:
My Jesus, that is best—that word being given
By the majestic angel whose command
Was softly, as a man's beseeching, said,
When I and all the earth appeared to stand
    In the great overflow
Of light celestial from his wings and head.
    Sleep, sleep, my saving One.

ELIZABETH BARRETT BROWNING

The days, the doubts, the dreams of pain
Are over, not to come again,
And from the menace of the night
Has dawned the day-star of delight:
My baby lies against me pressed—
Thus, Mother of God, are mothers blessed!

His little head upon my arm,
His little body soft and warm,
His little feet that cannot stand
Held in the heart of this my hand,
His little mouth close on my breast—
Thus, Mary's Son, are mothers blessed.

All dreams of deeds, all deeds of day
Are very faint and far away,
Yet you some day will stand upright

And fight God's foes, in manhood's might,
You—tiny, worshipped, clasped, caressed—
Thus, Mother of God, are mothers blessed.

Whatever grief may come to be
This hour divine goes on for me.
All glorious is my little span,
Since I, like God, have made a man,
A little image of God's best—
Thus, Mary's Son, are mothers blessed.

Come change, come loss, come worlds of tears,
Come endless chain of empty years;
They cannot take away the hour
That gives me You—my bird, my flower!
Thank God for this! Leave God the rest!—
Thus, Mother of God, are mothers blessed.

E. Nesbit

No sudden thing of glory and fear
Was the Lord's coming; but the dear
Slow Nature's days followed each other
To form the Saviour from His Mother
—One of the Children of the year.
The earth, the rain, received the trust
—The sun and dews, to frame the Just.
He drew His daily life from these,
According to His own decrees
Who makes man from the fertile dust.
Sweet summer and the winter wild,
These brought Him forth, the Undefiled.
The happy Springs renewed again
His daily bread, the growing grain,
The food and raiment of the Child.

ALICE MEYNELL

Sometimes, in quiet mood, I fancy, He
Sweet confidence told at Mary's knee.
There childish griefs, if such He had, grew less,
Or, fading out, made room for happiness.
He loved her much, and told her often, too;
And she? She pressed Him close, as mothers do.

The Madonna

With his kind Mother, who partakes thy woe,
Joseph, turn back: see, where your Child doth sit
Blowing, yea, blowing out those sparks of wit,
Which himself on those doctors did bestow.
The Word but lately could not speak; and lo,
It suddenly speaks wonders. Whence comes it,
That all which was, and all which would be, writ
A shallow-seeming Child should deeply know?
His Godhead was not soul to his Manhood;
Nor had time mellowed him to this ripeness;
But, as for one which hath long tasks, 'tis good
With the sun to begin his business,
He, in his age's morning, thus began
By miracles exceeding power of man.

JOHN DONNE

Herself a rose, who bore the Rose,
    She bore the Rose and felt its thorn,
    All Loveliness new-born
Took on her bosom its repose,
    And slept and woke there night and morn.

Lily herself, she bore the one
    Fair Lily; sweeter, whiter, far
    Than she or others are:
The Sun of Righteousness her Son,
    She was His morning star.

She gracious, He essential Grace,
    He was the Fountain, she the rill:
    Her goodness to fulfil
And gladness, with proportioned pace
    He led her steps thro' good and ill.

Christ's mirror she of grace and love,
    Of beauty and of life and death:
    By hope and love and faith
Transfigured to His Likeness "Dove
    Spouse, Sister, Mother," Jesus saith.

CHRISTINA ROSSETTI

WHEN JESUS SAW HIS MOTHER AND THE DISCIPLE WHOM HE LOVED STANDING BESIDE HER, HE SAID TO HIS MOTHER, "WOMAN, HERE IS YOUR SON." THEN HE SAID TO THE DISCIPLE, "HERE IS YOUR MOTHER." AND FROM THAT HOUR THE DISCIPLE TOOK HER INTO HIS OWN HOME.

JOHN 19:16–18, 26–27

His Mother cannot reach His face;

She stands in helplessness beside;

Her heart is martyred with her Son's;

Jesus, our Love, is crucified.

F. W. FABER

Oh! on what a sea of sorrow
    Was the Virgin-Mother cast,
When her eyes with tears o'erflowing
    Gazed upon her Son aghast,
From the bloodstained gibbet taken,
    Dying in her arms at last.

In her bitter desolation,
    His sweet mouth, His bosom too,
Then His riven side beloved,
    Then each hand, both wounded through,
Then His feet, with blood encrimsoned,
    Her maternal tears bedew.

She, a hundred times and over,
 Strains Him closely to her breast
Heart to Heart, arms arms enfolding,
 Are His wounds on her impressed:
Thus, in sorrow's very kisses,
 Melts her anguished soul to rest.

Oh, dear Mother! we beseech thee,
 By the tears thine eyes have shed,
By the cruel death of Jesus
 And His wounds' right royal red,
Make our hearts o'erflow with sorrow
 From thy heart's deep fountainhead.

To the Father, Son, and Spirit,
 Now we bend on equal knee:
Glory, sempiternal glory,
 To the Most High Trinity;
Yea! perpetual praise and honor
 Now and through all ages be.

ASCRIBED TO THE SERVITE,
CALLISTO PALUMBELLA

The Father saith, "Welcome, my Daughter":
   Saith the Spirit, "Welcome, my Spouse":
What have angels and archangels brought her?
   Stars for her brows.

"Welcome, Mother," the Son saith only,
   "Welcome, Mother." The years were slow
While she waited—the years were lonely—
   The summons to go.

Twelve long years of winter and summer,
   Feeding patient his altar light,
Michael tarried—the lordly comer
   Whose torch was bright.

Now, the Three in Unity claim her
   Close to each in the tenderest bond;
Now, the Three in Unity name her
   Holy and fond.

Now, the angels float from the azure,
   Kiss her feet and her mantle's rim;

She looks up at her Son, her Treasure,
     Hungry for Him.

Little feet that were wont to falter,
     Little fingers her lips once kissed:
Ages, spaces, His will can alter,
     Yea, as He list.

Mother of Christ, and all men's Mother,
     Where thou sittest the stars between,
Pluck His robe for His toiling brother
     Stricken with sin.

Yea, the strong desire of His Passion:
     Yea, the fruit of His mortal pain—
Intercede for thy mournful nation,
     Mother of men.

Intercede for thy mournful nation
     Toiling, stricken, seething beneath—
Yea, the strong desire of His Passion
     Bought with His Death.

KATHERINE TYNAN

*H*ail Mary, full of grace,

the Lord is with you!

Blessed are you among women,

and blessed is the fruit of your womb, Jesus.

Holy Mary, Mother of God,

pray for us sinners,

now and at the hour of our death.

Amen.

KNOWN AS "THE ANGELIC SALUTATION",
THIS PRAYER IS BASED ON LUKE 1:28,42

Memorare

Remember, most loving Virgin Mary,
never was it heard that anyone who turned
to you for help was left unaided.

Inspired by this confidence, though burdened
by my sins, I run to your protection
for you are my mother.

Mother of the Word of God,
do not despise my words of pleading
but be merciful and hear my prayer.

Amen.

This is a sixteenth-century version of
a prayer that was written in the fifteenth
century, perhaps by Saint Bernard

We turn to you for protection,
holy Mother of God.
Listen to our prayers and help us
in our needs.
Save us from every danger,
glorious and blessed Virgin.

THE PRAYER, FOUND IN A GREEK PAPYRUS,
DATED TO ABOUT 300, IS THE
OLDEST KNOWN PRAYER TO THE VIRGIN

Salve, Regina

Hail, holy Queen, Mother of mercy,
   hail, our life, our sweetness, and our hope.
To you we cry, the children of Eve;
   to you we send up our sighs,
   mourning and weeping in this land of exile.
Turn, then, most gracious advocate,
   your eyes of mercy toward us;
   lead us home at last
   and show us the blessed fruit
   of your womb, Jesus:
O clement, O loving, O sweet Virgin Mary.

THE "SALVE, REGINA," ONE OF THE FOUR
MARIAN ANTIPHONS WHICH IS SUNG AT THE
NIGHT PRAYER, ACCORDING TO THE SEASON,
WAS WRITTEN IN THE ELEVENTH CENTURY

O Lord Jesus Christ, Our Mediator with the Father, who has appointed the most blessed Virgin, Your Mother, to be our Mother also and our Mediatrix before You; grant that whoever draws near to You to beseech any benefit, may rejoice to receive all things through her. Who lives and reigns with God the Father and the Holy Spirit, forever and ever. Amen.

Prayer to Our Lady of the Barrio

O Queen of the Holy Rosary, Sweet Lady of Fatima, who hast deigned to appear in the land of Portugal and who hast restored peace to that country once in such turmoil, we beseech thee, look graciously upon our beloved country, and by thy power strengthen it spiritually and morally. Bring back peace, also, to all the peoples of the earth, so that all nations, especially our own, may rejoice to hail thee as their Queen, and as their Queen of Peace. Amen.

PRAYER TO OUR LADY OF FATIMA

Hail, holy Lady,
Most holy Queen,
Mary, Mother of God,
Ever Virgin;
Chosen by the most holy Father in heaven,
Consecrated by him,
With his most holy beloved Son
And the Holy Spirit, the comforter.
On you descended and in you still remains
All the fullness of grace
And every good.
Hail, his Palace.
Hail, his Tabernacle.
Hail, his Robe.
Hail, his Handmaid.
Hail, his Mother.
And hail, all holy virtues,
Who, by the grace
And inspiration of the Holy Spirit,
Are poured into the hearts of the faithful
So that, faithless no longer,
They may be made faithful servants of God
through you.

SAINT FRANCIS OF ASSISI

"Mother of God," some hope I find

In that remembered word.

Thou, on whose heart the sweet child lay

Who brought thy heart the sorrow,

Didst thou not see my little son?

Didst thou not smile to greet him?

With kisses on thy mouth didst run

To welcome him and greet him?

W. J. Dawson

At morn, at noon, at twilight dim,
Maria, thou hast heard my hymn:
In joy and woe, in good and ill,
Mother of God, be with me still.
When the hours flew brightly by,
And not a cloud obscured the sky,
My soul, lest it should truant be,
Thy grace did guide to thine and thee.
Now, when storms of fate o'ercast
Darkly my present and my past,
Let my future radiant shine
With sweet hopes of thee and thine.

EDGAR ALLEN POE

ONE MOTHER

Mary!
  I'm quite alone in all the world,
Into such bright sharp pain of anguish hurled
I cannot pray wise comfortable things;
Death's plunged me deep in hell, and given me wings
For terrible strange vastnesses; no hand
In all this empty spirit-driven space; I stand
Alone, and whimpering in my soul. I plod
Among wild stars, and hide my face from God.
God frightens me. He's strange. I know him not.
And all my usual prayers I have forgot:
But you—you had a son—I remember now!
You are not Mary of the virgin brow!
You agonized for Jesus! You went down
Into the ugly depths for him. Your crown
Is my crown! I've seen you in the street,
Begging your way for broken bread and meat:
I've seen you in trams, in shops, among old faces,
Young eyes, brave lips, broad backs, in all the places

Where women work, and weep, in pain, in pride.
Your hands were gnarled that held him when he died!
Not the fair hands that painters give you, white
And slim. You never had such hands: night
And day you labored, night and day, from child
To woman. You were never soft and mild,
But strong-limbed, patient, brown-skinned from the sun,
Deep-bosomed, brave-eyed, holy, holy One!
I know you now! I seek you, Mary! Spread
You compassionate skirts! I bring to you my dead!
You'll know him when you see him: first of all
Because he'll smile that way he did when he was small;
And then his eyes! They never changed from blue
To duller gray, as other children's do,
But like his childish dreams he kept his eyes
Vivid, and deeply clear, and visions wise.
Seek for him, Mary! Bright among the ghosts
Of other women's sons he'll star those hosts
Of shining boys! (He always topped his class
At school!) Lean forward, Mary, as they pass,

And touch him! When you see his eyes you'll weep
And this him your own Jesus! Let him sleep
In your deep bosom, Mary, then you'll see
His lashes, how they curl, so childishly
You'll weep again, and rock him on your heart
As I did once, that night we had to part.
He'll come to you all bloody and bemired,
And very shy. If he'd come home to me
I wouldn't ask the neighbors in to tea . . .
He always hated crowds . . . I'd let him be. . . .

And then perhaps you'll take him by the hand
And comfort him from fear when he must stand
Before God's dreadful throne; then, will you call
That boy whose bullet made my darling fall,
And take him by the other hand, and say. . .
" O God, whose Son the hands of men did slay,
These are Thy children who do take away

   The sins of the world. . . . "

                          IRENE RUTHERFORD MCLEOD

Blest Mother of my Lord, I fly to thee,
Who ever hast a mother's love for me,
Who prayest ceaselessly to God for me.

Thou Queen, who givest gifts of light to me,
In joy and weariness I turn to thee,
Lifting my hands and all my heart to thee.

No love of Jesus is flame-winged like thine,
For all His overflowing Heart is thine;
My Mother Mary, make thy Jesus mine.

HENRY A. RAWES

When evening shades are falling

O'er ocean's sunny sleep,

To pilgrims' hearts recalling

Their home beyond the deep;

When rest, o'er all descending,

The shores with gladness smile,

And lutes, their echoes blending,

Are heard from isle to isle:

Then, Mary, Star of the Sea,

We pray, we pray, to thee.

THOMAS MOORE

In all this history we see the picture of a woman belonging to that rare and beautiful class who approach the nearest to our ideal of angelic excellence. We see a woman in whom the genius and fire of the poet and prophetess is tempered by a calm and equable balance of the intellect; a woman not only to feel deeply, but to examine calmly and come to just results, and to act with energy befitting every occasion. Hers are the powers which might, in the providence of God, have had a public mission, but they are all concentrated in the nobler, yet secret mission of the mother. She lived and acted in her son, not in herself. Mary never seems to have sought to present herself as a public teacher; and in the one instance when she sought her son in public, it was from the tremulous anxiety of a mother's affection rather than the self-assertion of a mother's pride. Mary is presented to us as the mother, and the mother alone, seeking no other sphere. Like a true mother she passed out of self into her son, and the life that she lived was in him; and in this sacred self-abnegation she must forever remain, the one ideal type of perfect motherhood.

HARRIET BEECHER STOWE

*S*he . . . had no peer

Either in our first mother or in all women

Who were to come. But alone of all her sex

She pleased the Lord.

Caelius Sedulius

Passing
this Book
on to Dot Benson
10-1-99

Keep Well - dear Friend ♡JE

Keep

To Mother Lucille
From San Joseph
11/13/95